**Brighton & Hove City Council**

# BRIGHTON & HOVE CITY LIBRARIES

G000162495

## 24 hour renewal service via

www.citylibraries.info

or tel: 0303 123 0035

## To renew please have ready:

- Your library card number
- Your PIN for online, automated and self -service transactions

04503628

# WHATEVER HAPPENED

## TO...

# THE ANCIENT EGYPTIANS?

## BY KIRSTY HOLMES

**BookLife PUBLISHING**

©2019
BookLife Publishing Ltd.
King's Lynn
Norfolk, PE30 4LS

Written by:
Kirsty Holmes

Edited by:
John Wood

Designed by:
Dan Scase

# BC AND AD

In this book, you will see **BC** after and **AD** before some dates.
And some of the dates might look backwards. What's going on?

**AD** stands for **Anno Domini** and that means 'in the year of the Lord'.
Christian calendars count forwards from the year that Christians believe Jesus
Christ was born. When you see AD, you are counting forwards on the timeline.
**AD 1750 = 1750 years after Jesus was born.**

**BC** stands for **Before Christ.** If you see this next to a date, it means this
happened before the birth of Jesus Christ. When you see BC, you are
counting backwards on the timeline.
**1750 BC = 1750 years before Jesus was born.**

When describing a range of dates, you always count forwards.
So "between 1500 and 500 BC" or "from AD 500 to AD 1500" is correct.

**Check back here if you need to.**

2000 BC        1500 BC        1000 BC        500 BC

JESUS

WRITE THE
YEAR AND
THEN BC

# CONTENTS

PAGE 4    WHATEVER HAPPENED TO THE ANCIENT EGYPTIANS?

PAGE 6    WHO WERE THE ANCIENT EGYPTIANS?

PAGE 8    THE OLD KINGDOM AND THE NEW

PAGE 10    WHO, WHAT, WHEN, WHERE, HOW?

PAGE 12    PERSIAN INVADERS!

PAGE 14    ALEXANDER THE GREAT

PAGE 16    PTOLEMY, PTOLEMY, PTOLEMY...

PAGE 18    CLEOPATRA & CAESAR

PAGE 20    CLEOPATRA & MARK ANTONY

PAGE 22    WHAT THE ROMANS DID

PAGE 24    NEW GOD ON THE BLOCK

PAGE 26    A SLOW DECLINE

PAGE 28    WHAT REMAINS OF THE ANCIENTS?

PAGE 30    GLOSSARY

PAGE 32    INDEX

WORDS THAT LOOK LIKE <u>THIS</u> ARE EXPLAINED IN THE GLOSSARY ON PAGES 30 AND 31.

BORN

AD 500    AD 1000    AD 1500    AD 2000

WRITE AD AND THEN THE YEAR

# WHATEVER HAPPENED TO THE ANCIENT EGYPTIANS?

## MUMMY, CAN WE GO?

When you think of ancient Egypt, you are probably thinking of pyramids, mummies and very important cats. But if you went to Egypt today, you wouldn't be able to go to tea with the pharaoh or see anyone being mummified. Modern Egypt is a very different place. But why is that? Where did the **CULTURE**, people and traditions of one of the world's most **ICONIC** civilisations go?

I MEAN, AS GODS GO, I, SETH, AM ONE OF THE COOLEST. WHAT HAPPENED TO ME? HELLO?

CAIRO, AD 2018 / GIZA, 2560 BC

4

## OUT WITH THE OLD AND IN WITH THE NEW

It's easy to forget that ancient peoples were just like us in many ways. They had families, jobs, homes and leaders, just like we do. But the art, laws, history, lifestyle and beliefs they had back then could be very different. I bet you don't think you'll ever be made into a mummy — and I wonder what the ancient Egyptians would have thought about our modern computers? In this book, we will take a look at how the world of ancient Egypt ended, and where all their things might have gone...

THEY DON'T MAKE 'EM LIKE THEY USED TO ANY MORE. IN FACT, THEY DON'T MAKE MUMMIES AT ALL!

WAIT, WHAT?
TO PRONOUNCE THIS WORD, SAY:
PHARAOH = FARE-OH

# TURN ➜ THE PAGES OF HISTORY!

# WHO WERE THE ANCIENT EGYPTIANS?

## WHERE ON EARTH?

**FAMOUS FOR:**

- **Farmers**
- **Builders**
- **ENGINEERS**

THIS IS A MURAL. IT SHOWS ANCIENT EGYPTIANS BRINGING IN THE HARVEST. PHEW! LOOKS LIKE HARD WORK.

## ANCIENT EGYPTIAN INVENTIONS

PAPYRUS (PAPER MADE OF REEDS)

WRITING (IN HIEROGLYPHS)

MUMMIES (GROSS BUT COOL)

6

# OH, GODS!

The gods represented different things in nature, such as storms or a good harvest. The people believed they could keep the gods happy by performing **RITUALS** and giving **OFFERINGS** and **SACRIFICES**.

## SOCIAL SUCCESS

The ancient Egyptians had a clear **SOCIAL ORDER**, where some people were considered more important than others. Slaves were at the bottom of the social order and the pharaoh was at the top. The gods were even higher, and came above everyone. You could almost call it a pyramid... Oh look! We did!

**GODS**

**PHARAOH**

**VIZIER, SENIOR OFFICIALS, HIGH PRIESTS AND NOBLES**

**SCRIBES**

SKILLED **ARTISANS** AND CRAFTSPEOPLE

PEASANT FARMERS AND WORKERS

SERVANTS AND SLAVES

WORSHIP ME, PUNY HUMANS! (DO THEY HAVE MICE IN THE AFTERLIFE?)

THE ANCIENT EGYPTIANS THOUGHT CATS WERE **SACRED** AND THEY WOULD SACRIFICE CATS TO KEEP THE GODS HAPPY. IMPORTANT PEOPLE WERE OFTEN BURIED ALONG WITH THEIR CATS, WHICH HAD BEEN MUMMIFIED TOO.

**WAIT, WHAT?**
TO PRONOUNCE THIS WORD, SAY: PAPYRUS = PA-PIGH-RUS

# THE OLD KINGDOM AND THE NEW

## AGE OF THE PYRAMIDS

**AROUND 2649 TO 2130 BC:** The Great Pyramids at Giza were built as Egyptian **ARCHITECTS** perfected their pyramid-building skills. The oldest and largest is the Pyramid of Khufu. Eventually, the Old Kingdom gave way to a system of rulers, and the great kings of this **ERA** were no more...

OOH! FANCY!

THEY MIGHT LOOK CRUMBLY NOW, BUT THE PYRAMIDS WOULD HAVE BEEN COVERED IN LIMESTONE AND WOULD HAVE LOOKED VERY IMPRESSIVE. CAN YOU SEE THE SMALL AMOUNT THAT HASN'T WORN AWAY OVER THE YEARS, RIGHT AT THE TOP?

A time of **CHAOS** followed, known as the First Intermediate Period.

## THE MIDDLE KINGDOM

**2030 TO 1650 BC:** Ancient Egypt was calmer and settled again. The Nile was full and flooded regularly, leaving behind rich soil which was great for farming. Egypt did well... until some kings split the country into two, and Egypt was invaded by their neighbours, the Hyksos.

Can you guess what the next bit was called? That's right — the Second Intermediate Period!

KING MENTUHOTEP II REUNITED EGYPT INTO ONE COUNTRY AGAIN.

# THE NEW KINGDOM

**1520 TO 1075 BC:** This was a time of wealth, good harvests and power, and this era produced some of the most famous pharaohs ever, such as Tutankhamun, Hatshepsut, and a whole bunch of kings called Ramesses...

IT WAS ALL GOING SO WELL. MY SON, RAMESSES III, WAS ON THE THRONE... HE SPENT ALL OUR MONEY ON WARS, AND THEN THE SKY GREW DARK AND NOTHING GREW.... I BLAME THE PARENTS... HANG ON! I AM THE PARENT!

SOME PEOPLE THINK THE DARKENED SKY WAS CAUSED BY A VOLCANO IN GREECE ERUPTING AND SPEWING TONNES AND TONNES OF ASH CLOUDS INTO THE SKY.

WAIT, WHAT?
TO PRONOUNCE THESE WORDS, SAY:
KHUFU = COO-FOO
HYKSOS = HICK-SOSS
MENTUHOTEP = MEN-TOO-HO-TEP
TUTANKHAMUN = TOOT-AN-CAR-MUN
HATSHEPSUT = HAT-SHEP-SUT
RAMESSES = RAM-SEES

THE LOVELY GREEK ISLAND OF SANTORINI

TERRIFYING, CROP-KILLING VOLCANO?

# WHO, WHAT, WHEN, WHERE, HOW?

Historians know a lot about ancient Egypt because so much of their stuff still exists, such as the pyramids, hieroglyphs and mummies. However, there are many things about ancient Egypt that historians still aren't sure about, such as how this great civilisation ended. Great civilisations, such as the Egyptians, tend to slowly fall from greatness over time. Ancient Egypt was invaded lots of times through the years, and each new invader brought their own rules, traditions, religions and customs with them.

HMM. A SERIES OF... UM... IMPORTANT-LOOKING ROCKS. THIS TELLS ME A LOT (I HOPE)...

HISTORIANS WHO STUDY ANCIENT EGYPT ARE CALLED EGYPTOLOGISTS.

Did ancient Egypt fall when the last **NATIVE** Egyptian ruler, King Nectanebo II, left the throne in 342 BC?

HEY! DON'T BLAME ME!

KING NECTANEBO II (HE'S IN THE SARCOPHAGUS)

Maybe it was when Egypt became a **PROVINCE** of the Roman Empire in 30 BC?

ALL OF EGYPT IS MINE!!

Or was it much later, when the last hieroglyphs were used?

THE EGYPTIANS WERE USING EMOJIS BEFORE THEY WERE COOL...

The final blow could have been when the main religion changed to Christianity and then Islam, and the old gods were forgotten.

WAIT, WHAT?
TO PRONOUNCE THESE WORDS, SAY:

NECTANEBO =
NEK-TA-NEB-O

SARCOPHAGUS =
SAR-COFF-A-GUS

We're going to look at the story of the slow fall of one of humanity's greatest-ever civilisations. And at the end, you can make up your own mind as to why it fell.

# PERSIAN INVADERS!

## 525 BC

Egypt had some very powerful neighbours. Over the centuries, it had been invaded by most of them. But some people argue that the invasion of the Persians marked the beginning of the end.

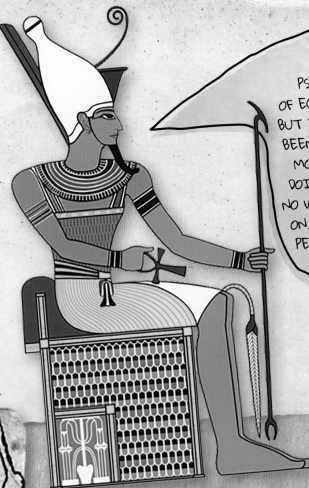

I AM KING PSAMTIK III, PHAROAH OF EGYPT. DON'T TELL ANYONE, BUT I'M A BIT NEW. I'VE ONLY BEEN PHARAOH FOR ABOUT SIX MONTHS, BUT I THINK I'M DOING PRETTY WELL, SO FAR. NO WARS, NO INVASIONS... HANG ON. WHAT'S THAT? OH NO! THE PERSIANS ARE COMING! GET THE CAMELS!

CAMBYSES II

Persian king Cambyses II invaded Egypt in 525 BC, eventually defeating Psamtik III at the battle of Pelusium. There are stories that say Cambyses ordered his warriors to paint pictures of the cat goddess Bastet on their shields, knowing that the Egyptians worshipped cats. Some even said he held cats in front of his army to stop the Egyptians from firing their arrows. The punishment in ancient Egypt for harming a cat was death.

Egypt became part of the Persian Empire. Cambyses II and a series of Persian kings ruled the country until 402 BC, when Egypt ruled itself again under a series of **DYNASTIES**. The last of these great ruling families was King Nectanebo II, who would go on to be the last ever native ruler of ancient Egypt.

Could this be the beginning of the end for the ancient Egyptians?

# ALEXANDER THE GREAT

Across the sea, there was Macedonia — a part of Northern Greece. They had one of the most famous kings ever, and he was called Alexander. The young king Alexander would come to be known as Alexander the Great, because of everything he did in his short life. He invaded and conquered many countries as he swept across Europe and Asia, and one of them was Egypt. Alexander was thought to be a hero as he **LIBERATED** Egypt from Persian rule.

THERE IS NOTHING IMPOSSIBLE TO HIM WHO WILL TRY! NOW BUILD A CITY AND NAME IT AFTER ME!

Egypt might have thought it was saved – but was this just another step in its fall? In 305 BC, a man called Ptolemy took the throne of Egypt as pharaoh. But Ptolemy I was not Egyptian – he was Greek! The Ptolemies ruled Egypt for almost 300 years.

Egypt changed in lots of ways during the Ptolemaic dynasty. Greek soldiers had been given land, and so across the country, more and more Greek people settled and brought their culture with them. Alexander founded a new city, Alexandria, in the Greek style, and although the culture of the Egyptians carried on, there was an unmistakably Greek feel...

**THE FAMOUS LIGHTHOUSE AT ALEXANDRIA**

THIS STUFF DOESN'T LOOK EGYPTIAN AT ALL!

**WAIT, WHAT?**
TO PRONOUNCE THESE WORDS, SAY:

MACEDONIA =
MASS-EH-DOH-NEE-AH

PTOLEMAIC =
TOLL-A-MAY-IK

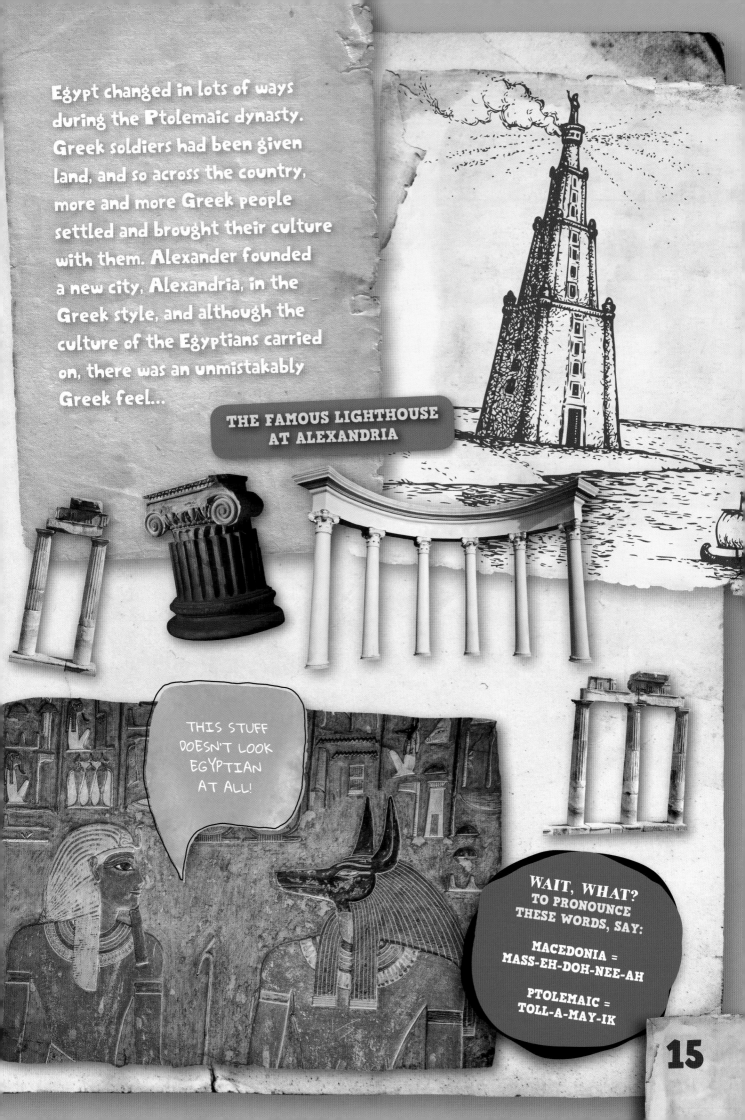

# PTOLEMY, PTOLEMY, PTOLEMY...

## KEEP IT IN THE FAMILY

The Ptolemy family was a strange one. All the men were called Ptolemy, and all the women were called either Cleopatra, Berenice or Arsinoe! The Ptolemies only married their own **SIBLINGS** in order to keep the family as royal as could be.

NO NEED TO LEARN TO SPEAK THE LANGUAGE OF THIS WEIRD COUNTRY - EVEN IF I AM PHARAOH! I'LL JUST LIVE HERE IN ALEXANDRIA WHERE EVERYTHING IS VERY GREEK - JUST THE WAY I LIKE IT!

PTOLEMY I OF EGYPT

The first two Ptolemaic kings, Ptolemy I and II, were good kings. After that, things got a bit shaky. The next few Ptolemies brought war to Egypt. As could be expected when siblings have to live together, there was a lot of in-fighting in the family. There was even a **CIVIL WAR**. Egypt was left weakened by Ptolemaic rule, as the family focussed on their own problems and forgot to, well, rule...

PTOLEMY VIII

I AM THE EGYPTIAN GOD OF CHAOS! AND EVERYTHING SEEMS TO BE WORKING OUT!

**WAIT, WHAT?**
TO PRONOUNCE THESE WORDS, SAY:

CLEOPATRA = CLEE-OH-PAT-RAH
BERENICE = BEAR-UH-NEESE
ARSINOE = AR-SIN-OH-WAY

SETH, EGYPTIAN GOD OF CHAOS

17

# CLEOPATRA & CAESAR

## QUEEN OF KINGS

The last Ptolemaic ruler was probably the most famous. Queen Cleopatra was a great queen, and more loved by the people of Egypt than the rest of her family – for a start, she actually learned the language! She is known as not only a great beauty, but as a charming and very intelligent leader.

THE NAME CLEOPATRA MEANS "GLORY OF THE FATHER".

## HAIL, CAESAR!

Cleopatra decided she didn't need her husband (who was also her 12-year-old brother, Ptolemy XIII) in order to rule, so they were at war. When the Roman leader Julius Caesar came to Egypt, legend tells that Cleopatra smuggled herself in to see him, rolled up in a carpet. Caesar was so taken with her beauty and brains that they immediately began an **AFFAIR**. Caesar took control of Alexandria from Cleopatra's husband and then restored Cleopatra to the throne.

FINALLY, I AM PROPERLY QUEEN OF EGYPT! I AM THE NEW <u>INCARNATION</u> OF THE GODDESS ISIS. I CAN GET ON WITH BEING THE EXCELLENT RULER THAT I WAS CLEARLY BORN TO BE. NOW TO TELL CAESAR THAT I'M PREGNANT WITH HIS CHILD...

STABBED TO DEATH IN MY OWN <u>SENATE</u>! I GUESS THAT'S WHAT YOU GET FOR BEING TOO POWERFUL.

## LET'S GO!

The child, called **Caesarion** (meaning 'little **Caesar**') was an important link between the **Egyptian** and **Roman** empires. **Cleopatra** went to Rome and spent some years with **Caesar** as he rose to power. She needed his power to keep her throne, and he needed her money and grain supplies. It was all going well until **Caesar** was killed...

# CLEOPATRA & MARK ANTONY

## AN AFFAIR TO REMEMBER

**P**tolemy **XIII** died, leaving **Cleopatra** as the ruler of Egypt. **Cleopatra** was a powerful queen by now. She visited the powerful Roman leader **Marcus Antonius** (**Mark Antony**). Instead of hiding in a carpet, she went, dressed as goddess **APHRODITE**, in a ship with silver oars and splendid purple sails. They also began an affair and had three children. **Cleopatra** was named the Queen of Kings — an extremely high honour. Surely Egypt was now safe?

MARCUS ANTONIUS

89

96

I'M OCTAVIAN, AND I HATE CLEOPATRA AND HER SON. I AM AT WAR WITH EGYPT NOW, AND MARCUS ANTONIUS HAS SIDED WITH CLEOPATRA! I FOUND HIS SECRET **WILL** (WELL, I STOLE IT) AND IT SAYS THAT HE'S GOING TO GIVE ROMAN TERRITORY TO CLEOPATRA WHEN HE DIES! I CAN'T LET THAT HAPPEN. I'LL HAVE TO TAKE OVER AND BECOME <u>DICTATOR.</u>

**OCTAVIAN, CAESAR'S ADOPTED SON**

Antony and Cleopatra fought a great battle with Octavian's forces, but they had to flee. They were defeated in Alexandria a few days later. Marcus Antonius fell onto his own sword and died in Cleopatra's arms. A few days later, she also died. Some say she killed herself by allowing a poisonous snake to bite her. She was the last of the pharaohs, and one of the most powerful women in history. Did ancient Egypt die with her that day?

**DID A SNAKE BRING DOWN THE EGYPTIANS?**

**EGYPTIAN COBRA**

# WHAT THE ROMANS DID

## ROMANI VENTURUS ES**

By 30 BC, Egypt had become a province of the Roman Empire. Without the rule of a pharaoh, the Roman emperors were in charge, and they quickly set about making things as Roman as they could. Egypt became a great grain producer, growing grain for the empire in Egypt's excellent farms. Life at the top was very different from the rule of Khufu and Nectanebo.

** THIS MEANS 'THE ROMANS ARE COMING' IN LATIN, THE LANGUAGE THE ROMANS SPOKE.

OBELISK

THE ROMANS BECAME FASCINATED BY THE HISTORY OF THEIR NEW PROVINCE. OBELISKS LIKE THIS ONE WERE BUILT IN ROME. WAS EGYPTIAN CULTURE DYING... OR WAS IT ACTUALLY COMING BACK?

## A MELTING POT

Just as Egyptian culture spread throughout the Roman Empire, the Roman way of life crept into Egypt too. The Egyptian people started adopting **GRECO-ROMAN** culture in their own art, religion and ways of life. But the Egyptian people were still using hieroglyphs, making mummies, and building temples to the old gods. If Roman rule could not end these ancient cultures and practices, then where **DID** they go?

# NEW GOD ON THE BLOCK

BASTET

HELLO? HELLO? ANYONE THERE?

## HAVE YOU HEARD THE WORD?

Christianity was on the rise. This religion had only been around for a few hundred years, and Christians had been **PERSECUTED** and even outlawed during that time. Constantine I made sure it was no longer illegal to be Christian, and over the next 100 years, Christianity spread. Slowly, the old gods were being lost and replaced as Christian emperors ruled and the old temples crumbled and were forgotten.

Egyptian religion had survived for thousands of years. It had changed over that time, but the worship of the old gods had carried on through invasions by many different people. Christianity, a once secret and persecuted religion, could flourish and grow, first in Alexandria, then slowly out to the Egyptian people. While other religions over time had been able to exist alongside the old Egyptian gods, Christianity was clear: there was to be no god but their God. People stopped looking after the temples, and slowly the old beliefs faded away...

NOOOOOOOOO........

## WHAT DOES THIS FISH MEAN AGAIN?

As the old religions faded away, so did many other things from ancient Egyptian culture. Hieroglyphs were not needed any more, and Christianity had no room for mummification or sacrifices. It wasn't even particularly fond of cats...

SAD TIMES.

# A SLOW DECLINE

## MILLENNIA, NOT MOMENTS

As you can see, great civilisations take hundreds or thousands of years to become great. And the bigger they are, the harder – or indeed, slower – they fall. It's hard to stick a pin in a timeline and say: that's the moment ancient Egypt ended. But we're going to try anyway...

Time to put your Egyptologist hat on and ask yourself:
**WHATEVER HAPPENED TO THE ANCIENT EGYPTIANS?**

**2181 BC:**
Did ancient Egypt end with the fall of the Old Kingdom?

**525 BC:**
Or was it all over when the Persians invaded?

**342 BC:**
Maybe the end came when the last native ruler lost the throne?

It's up to you, young historian. Which moment do you think truly brought down the ancient Egyptians?

CLEOPATRA

**305 BC:**
Was the rule of the Greeks the final blow, with Ptolemy I?

**30 BC:**
Did ancient Egypt die with its last pharaoh, Cleopatra?

**AD 300:**
When the old gods left the people behind, did they take ancient Egypt with them?

**AD 400 – 500:**
No more hieroglyphs, mummies or sacred cats = no more ancient Egypt?

# WHAT REMAINS OF THE ANCIENTS?

## A TOMB WITH A VIEW...

KHUFU PROBABLY NEVER IMAGINED THIS VIEW!

Egypt today is a modern place, with bustling cities and a thriving culture all of its own. But if you travel to modern-day Giza, the pyramid of Khufu stands tall over the edge of the city. Ancient Egypt may be no more, but modern Egypt is a country that still honours and remembers its rich history. We've seen what was lost, but let's look at what survived...

## EYE MAKEUP

THE EGYPTIANS INVENTED EYELINER, ALTHOUGH YOU MIGHT NOT HAVE WANTED TO WEAR IT. IT WAS MADE OF LEAD, WHICH PROTECTED THE EYE FROM INFECTIONS... BUT WAS ALSO VERY POISONOUS!

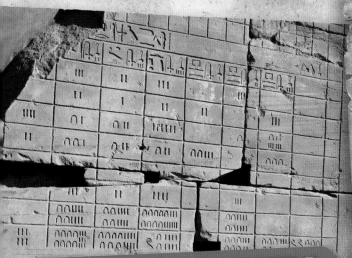

AN ANCIENT EGYPTIAN CALENDAR ON THE WALL AT THE TEMPLE OF KARNAK IN LUXOR

## 365 DAYS

The Egyptians relied on the flooding of the Nile, so knowing when this would happen helped them to plan their farming seasons. The Egyptians were the first to develop the 365-day calendar, based on the phases of the moon. We still use this system today.

## PAPER...

PAPYRUS WAS A MAT WOVEN FROM REEDS, THEN POUNDED FLAT TO MAKE A SURFACE THAT COULD BE WRITTEN ON. IT'S ALSO THE FIRST PAPER WE KNOW OF ANYWHERE IN THE WORLD!

## ...PENS

ANCIENT EGYPTIAN REED PENS IN THEIR WOODEN PENCIL CASES

It makes sense that the people who invented the first paper also invented the first pens!

## THE PLOUGH

EGYPTIANS DIDN'T INVENT THE PLOUGH, BUT BEFORE THEY CAME ALONG IT COULD TAKE FOUR MEN TO HAUL A PLOUGH THROUGH THE SOIL. NOT THE CLEVER EGYPTIANS, THOUGH: THEY USED THE STRENGTH OF AN OX TO PULL THEIR PLOUGHS.

# GLOSSARY

**AFFAIR**

when a person has a secret relationship with someone but is already married to someone else

**APHRODITE**

ancient Greek goddess of love and beauty

**ARCHITECTS**

people who design buildings

**ARTISANS**

people skilled in making things

**CHAOS**

something that has no order

**CIVIL WAR**

a war between different groups in the same country

**CULTURE**

the way of life and traditions of a group of people

**DICTATOR**

a ruler who has all the power and runs the country on their own

**DYNASTIES**

clear lines of rulers who are related to each other

**ENGINEERS**

people who plan or build machines or structures to a specific design

**ERA**

a period of time in history

**GRECO-ROMAN**

connected to or in the style of the Greeks and Romans

**HIEROGLYPHS**

a type of writing used by ancient Egyptians

**ICONIC**

when something is well known and a symbol of a place or time

## INCARNATION

a form taken, usually by a god or goddess

## LIBERATED

freed or let out

## NATIVE

a person born in a certain place

## OFFERINGS

things offered as gifts to a god or gods, usually in the hopes of pleasing them

## PAGAN

the Roman and Greek style of religion which had many gods that represented different things

## PERSECUTED

treated very badly because of race or beliefs

## PROVINCE

an area that belongs to a certain country but is not in that country

## RITUALS

ordered actions that take place during religious ceremonies

## SACRED

connected to gods or goddesses

## SACRIFICES

objects or living things that are destroyed to please the gods

## SARCOPHAGUS

a stone coffin

## SENATE

a group of people in Roman times who helped run the Roman Empire and create laws

## SIBLINGS

brothers or sisters in a family

## SOCIAL ORDER

a system in which some people are more important than others

## VIZIER

an important official in a government

## WILL

a written document that explains what someone wants to happen to their things after they die

# INDEX

**A**

**Alexander the Great** 14
**Alexandria, city of** 15–16, 18, 21, 25
**Antonius, Marcus (Mark Antony)** 12, 20–21

**C**

**Caesar, Julius** 18–19, 21
**Caesarion** 19
**Cambyses** 12–13
**cats** 4, 7, 12, 25, 27
**Christianity** 2, 11, 24–25
**Constantine the Great** 24
**culture** 4, 15, 22–23, 25, 28

**E**

**Egyptologists** 10, 26
**gods** 4, 7, 11–12, 17, 19–20, 23–25, 27
- **Aphrodite (Greek)** 20
- **Bastet** 12, 24
- **Isis** 19, 23
- **Seth** 4, 17

**H**

**hieroglyphics** 6, 10–11, 23, 25, 27
**Hyksos** 8–9

**I**

**Islam** 11

**M**

**mummies** 4–7, 10, 23, 27

**O**

**Octavian** 21

**P**

**papyrus** 7, 29
**Persians** 12–14, 26
**Pharoahs** 4, 7, 9, 12, 14, 16, 21–22, 27
- **Cleopatra** 16–21, 27
- **Hatshepsut** 9
- **Khufu** 8, 22, 28
- **Mentuhotep** 8–9
- **Nectanebo** 10–11, 13, 22
- **Psamtik** 12–13
- **Ptolemy** 14, 16–18, 27
- **Ramesses** 9
- **Tutankhamun** 9
**pyramids** 4, 7–8, 10, 28

**R**

**River Nile** 8, 29

# PHOTO CREDITS

All images are courtesy of Shutterstock.com, unless otherwise specified. With thanks to Getty Images, Thinkstock Photo and iStockphoto. Front Cover – Yevgen Kotyukh, Jose Ignacio Soto, spaxiax, Dean Drobot, Merydolla, Nadya_Art. 4&5 – Abdoabdalla, Skreidzeleu, tan_tan, Studio 37, worker. 6&7 – Jose Ignacio Soto, jsp, farres, Juanan Barros Moreno, GSK, Ttatty, Andrea Izzotti. 6&7 – givaga, NebMaatRa, agsaz, Metropolitan Museum of Art. 8&9 – givaga, NebMaatRa, agsaz, Metropolitan Museum of Art. 10&11 – cornfield, Rama, Cris Foto, FlavoredPixels, tan_tan, Aratehortua, NotionPic. 12&13 – tan_tan, Macrovector, Jakub Hałun. 14&15 – Lambros Kazan, Stella, Jakub Kyncl, In Green. 16&17 – Karen Green, Vladimir Zadvinskii. 18&19 – Fat Jackey, burnel1, lynea. 20&21 – Ancientrome.ru, MariMarkina, Eric Isselee. 22&23 – LifeCollectionPhotography, Thalo. 24&25 – aSuruwataRi, Andrea Izzotti. 26&27 – Internet Archive Book Images, rowanwindwhistler, Wellcome Images. 28&29 – Raimonds Romans raymoonds, FlexDreams, Nadya Korobkova. Paper – ZaZa Studio, Monica Butnaru, Ints Vikmanis, ZaZa Studio, Anton Watman. Speech Bubbles – Nataleana. Caption banner – Olga_C